ALL YOU NEED IS A PENCIL

THE ← ← ← ← ← ← TOTALLY HILARIOUS ALL ABOUT AMERICA ACTIVITY BOOK

Activities, Games, Doodling Fun , Puzzles, and Much, Much, Much, Much More!

JOE RHATIGAN
ILLUSTRATIONS BY ANTHONY OWSLEY

imagine!

To my brother Tom, who liked social studies class a lot more than I did. —J.R.

An Imagine Book
Published by Charlesbridge
85 Main Street, Watertown, MA 02472
(617) 926-0329
www.charlesbridge.com

Text copyright © 2016 by Joseph Rhatigan
Illustrations copyright © 2016 by Charlesbridge Publishing, Inc.
Interior and cover design by Melissa Gerber
Printed in China, January 2016.

The publisher does not have any control over and does not assume any responsibility
for author or third-party websites or their content.

ISBN 978-1-62354-076-0
10 9 8 7 6 5 4 3 2 1

THANKS TO AMERICA . . . WE HAVE PENCILS WITH ERASERS!

America is known for many great accomplishments. We were the first to fly. We put the first people on the moon. We were the first to put peanut butter on our chocolate. But let's start off *All About America* by thanking one special American without whose special contribution this book wouldn't be possible: Hymen Lipman. Although you probably never heard of this Philadelphia inventor, in 1858 he received the first patent for attaching an eraser to the end of a pencil. Erasers already existed; so did pencils. Lipman was the genius who put them together.

Now that you're holding this book in your hands, the only other thing you'll need is one of Lipman's inventions! With pencil in hand, many fun, interesting, and wacky activities await— all of which have something to do with the United States of America. Will you learn anything? Of course you will! Will you have a blast? Absolutely.

So, put a feather in your cap, salute Old Glory, and let the fun begin!

The eraser end of Lipman's invention had to be sharpened just like the graphite end. Lipman sold his patent for one hundred thousand dollars, which was a good thing because the US Supreme Court ruled the invention un-patent-worthy in 1875.

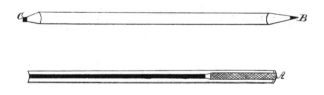

US Patent #19,783: Combination of lead pencil and eraser.

ALL ABOUT AMERICA

America wants to take this personality quiz. Can you help?
Answers on page 134.

1. Full name:

_____

2. Nicknames:

_____

3. Year of birth:

_____

4. Birthday:

_____

5. Names of America's parents:

_____

6. Number of America's family members:

_____

7. Neighbors:

_____

8. Favorite song:

_____

9. Favorite relative:

_____

10. Favorite animal:

_____

11. Favorite flower:

_____

12. Farthest traveled:

_____

13. Favorite tree:

_____

ALL ABOUT YOU

Imagine you are a country.

Full name:
_____

Nicknames:
_____

Year of birth:
_____

Birthday:
_____

National anthem:
_____

National animal:
_____

National flower:
_____

National tree:
_____

List other national symbols you would have:
_____

Design the flag for your country:

Tell the story of how your country came to be:

_____

_____

_____

_____

Who are the heroes of your country and why?

_____

_____

_____

_____

Describe the people who live in your country:

_____

_____

_____

_____

Explain some of the laws of your country:

_____

_____

_____

_____

How does your government work?

_____

_____

_____

How does your country deal with problems such as environmental issues, lack of resources, poverty, and more?

_____

_____

_____

_____

DON'T THINK TWICE: FOUNDING FATHERS EDITION

Answer the questions below as quickly as possible without putting too much thought into them. Time yourself and see how many you get right. Don't write in the book if you want to play with friends. **Answers on page 134.**

Scoring: Divide the number of seconds it took you to take the quiz by the number of questions you got correct. The lower your score, the better. For example, if it took you twenty seconds to get nine questions correctly answered, your score would be 2.2. If it took you twenty-five seconds to get all ten questions right, your score would be 2.5. So, in this case, speed was better than accuracy!

Hint: If you don't know an answer, skip it! Remember, the object of this quiz is not only to get as many correct answers as possible, but also to do it in as little time as possible.

1–3: Awesome!
4–6: Smarty-pants
7 & up: Not bad!

Fill in the blanks:

1. _____ Washington was our first president.

2. John _____ was our second president.

3. Thomas _____ was our third president.

4. John _____ had the biggest signature on the Declaration of Independence.

5. Ben _____ invented the lightning rod and was considered the First American.

6. Alexander _____ was our first Secretary of the Treasury and was killed in a duel.

7. James _____ was our fourth president and considered the Father of the Constitution.

8. _____ Jay was the first Chief Justice of the Supreme Court.

9. Patrick _____ gave the famous "Give me liberty or give me death" speech.

10. Samuel _____ was a leader in Massachusetts who helped push the colonies toward war with Great Britain.

A BIT OF LEARNIN'

What about the Founding Mothers? Focusing on just the men of the Revolution leaves half the story untold. For example, sixteen-year-old Sybil Ludington rode forty miles in New York State to spread the news of a British attack. She also rounded up four hundred militiamen to fight. (Paul Revere's ride was only sixteen miles, and he got caught!) Other Founding Mothers acted as spies, dressed as men and fought in battles, raised money for the army, and more.

DESIGN THE FLAG

The US flag has thirteen stripes, one for each of the thirteen British colonies that declared independence from Great Britain. It also has a grouping of fifty stars, one for each state in the Union. What would our flag look like if we had a different number of colonies and states?

10 original colonies and 40 states

3 original colonies and 20 states

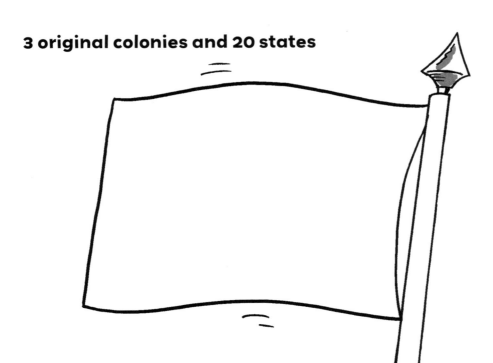

23 original colonies and 44 states

7 original colonies and 14 states

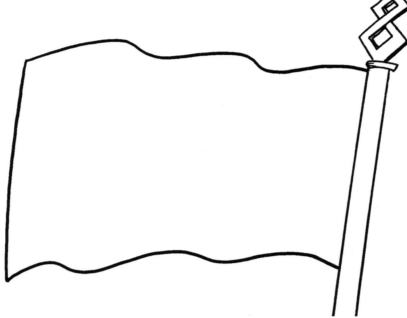

1 original colony and 1 state

What else might make a good flag to represent the United States? Design your own flag here:

A BIT OF LEARNIN'

Most historians agree that Betsy Ross did not design the original Stars and Stripes US flag. One account says her grandson made up the story one hundred years after the flag was designed.

STATES OF CONFUSION

Can you identify each of these US states by its outline? Hint: Not all of them are right-side up! **Answers on page 134.**

1. _____

2. _____

3. _____

4. _____

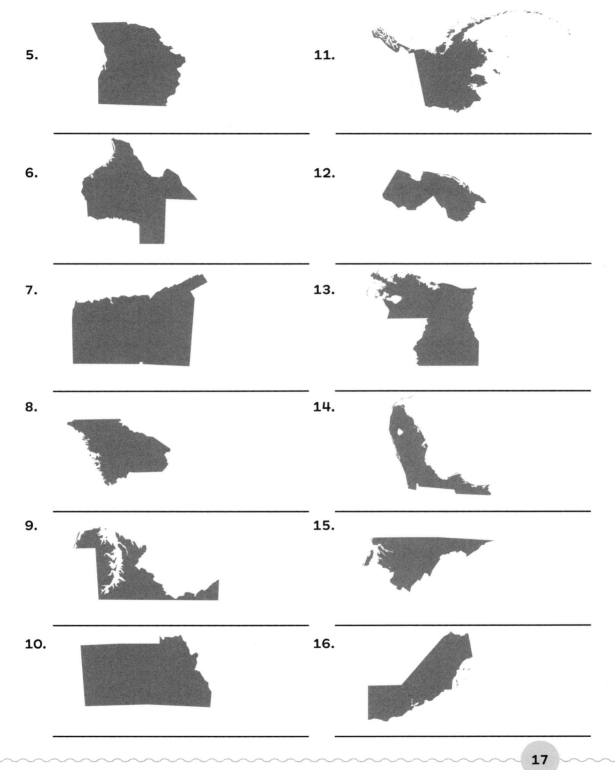

5. _____

6. _____

7. _____

8. _____

9. _____

10. _____

11. _____

12. _____

13. _____

14. _____

15. _____

16. _____

ABBREVIATION COMPLETION

Find the abbreviations of all fifty states in the sentences below. For example, see where the abbreviations for New York (NY) and Maryland (MD) are found in the following sentence: ANYone want to help MoM Decorate her new office? Each sentence has three or more states in it, and some states appear more than once.

Answers on page 134.

1. Washington pledged a solemn oath to defend the fledgling nation. Foreign nations that interfered with US matters would pay the price.

2. On November 2, 1983, President Ronald Reagan signed a bill declaring the third Monday of January a holiday honoring Martin Luther King, Jr.

3. That Xerox machine tends to break down just when I need to make a lot of copies.

4. My school's improv theater acting video gained many new viewers last week.

5. By midnight the only ones left at the vacation home were Mom, Dad, and me.

6. Tommy's dentist administered a new, very painful procedure. It made him ill and dazed, and now he can only lick yogurt for the rest of the day.

7. On cold days, I always enjoy the warmth of John's billowy green jacket. He asks me not to, but then he says, "Okay."

8. Whiskers squirms until I give him his catnap toy. He inhales it and then lies there unmoving.

Here are the states with their abbreviations. Mark them off once you find them.

ALABAMA	AL	MISSISSIPPI	MS
ALASKA	AK	MISSOURI	MO
ARIZONA	AZ	MONTANA	MT
ARKANSAS	AR	NEBRASKA	NE
CALIFORNIA	CA	NEVADA	NV
COLORADO	CO	NEW HAMPSHIRE	NH
CONNECTICUT	CT	NEW JERSEY	NJ
DELAWARE	DE	NEW MEXICO	NM
FLORIDA	FL	NEW YORK	NY
GEORGIA	GA	NORTH CAROLINA	NC
HAWAII	HI	NORTH DAKOTA	ND
IDAHO	ID	OHIO	OH
ILLINOIS	IL	OKLAHOMA	OK
INDIANA	IN	OREGON	OR
IOWA	IA	PENNSYLVANIA	PA
KANSAS	KS	RHODE ISLAND	RI
KENTUCKY	KY	SOUTH CAROLINA	SC
LOUISIANA	LA	SOUTH DAKOTA	SD
MAINE	ME	TENNESSEE	TN
MARYLAND	MD	TEXAS	TX
MASSACHUSETTS	MA	UTAH	UT
MICHIGAN	MI	VERMONT	VT
MINNESOTA	MN	VIRGINIA	VA
		WASHINGTON	WA
		WEST VIRGINIA	WV
		WISCONSIN	WI
		WYOMING	WY

YANKEE DOODLES

Famous people are sometimes known for a famous attribute or article of clothing. These are often made fun of or exaggerated in images of those people. Draw your own exaggerated items for the famous Americans below!

How tall is President Abraham Lincoln's hat?

How wide is Abigail Adams's dress?

President Teddy Roosevelt liked to say, "Speak softly and carry a big stick; you will go far." How big was Roosevelt's stick?

Five-star general Douglas MacArthur received the Medal of Honor and many other medals during his long career in the Army. How many medals did he have?

President Jimmy Carter was often portrayed with big teeth. How many teeth do you think he had?

A IS FOR AMERICA

The New-England Primer was the first reading textbook created for the American colonies. First published in the late 1600s, it was used to teach children to read, and more than two million copies were sold in the 1700s. The book introduced the letters of the alphabet with pictures and rhymes. For instance, here is the entry for D: A Dog will bite a thief at night.

Come up with your own alphabet rhymes below. You can choose a theme (America, favorite things, whatever!) or rhyme randomly. Then, find a little kid and teach him his ABCs!

A

_____

_____

_____

B

_____

_____

_____

C

_____

_____

_____

D

_____

_____

_____

E

_____

_____

_____

F

_____

_____

_____

G

_____

_____

_____

H

_____

_____

_____

I

_____

_____

_____

J

_____

_____

_____

K

_____

_____

_____

L

_____

_____

_____

M

_____

_____

_____

N

_____

_____

_____

O

_____

_____

_____

P

_____

_____

_____

Q

_____

_____

_____

R

_____

_____

_____

S

_____

_____

_____

T

_____

_____

_____

U

_____

_____

_____

V

_____

_____

_____

W

X

Y

Z

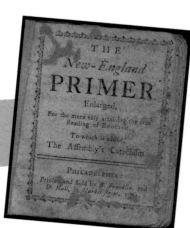

The inside cover of The New-England Primer printed by Ben Franklin in 1764.

MORE PRIMER FUN

Once they learned their ABCs, young colonists wrote sentences that started with the letters of the alphabet. Here's A: *A wise son makes a glad father, but a foolish son is the heaviness of his mother.* See if you can write sentences beginning with each letter of the alphabet. To make it even more interesting, try to make each sentence some form of advice.

A

_____

_____

B

_____

_____

C

_____

_____

D

_____

_____

E

_____

_____

F

_____

_____

G

_____

_____

H

_____

_____

I

_____

_____

J

_____

_____

K

_____

_____

L

_____

_____

M

_____

_____

N

O

P

Q

R

S

T

U

V

_____

_____

W

_____

_____

X

_____

_____

Y

_____

_____

Z

_____

_____

A BIT OF LEARNIN'

The New-England Primer was a mix of religious prayers and poems, which in some instances were all children had to read. Some of these prayers are still used today.

POPULAR MALE NAMES IN 1777

Can you find these twelve popular male first names from 1777 in the grid below? **Answers on page 135.**

Noadiah	Bartholomew	Zadock
Ozias	Barnabas	Uzzah
Shem	Barzillai	Xenophon
Theophilus	Peletiah	Ralph

```
Z  J  H  C  K  D  C  R  B  N  W  K  W  Z  L  K  R  F  K  G
F  U  W  G  M  H  E  A  N  L  P  L  C  I  N  K  S  D  A  E
T  L  Q  D  V  F  R  A  O  H  L  F  C  O  C  E  D  G  X  D
A  K  X  J  V  Z  C  X  H  I  O  Z  J  J  D  O  Q  I  J  U
N  O  A  D  I  A  H  I  P  B  A  R  N  A  B  A  S  H  E  M
Y  X  I  L  H  X  R  A  O  L  T  H  K  E  M  Y  Z  W  M  N
W  P  L  P  K  Z  G  U  N  H  Q  I  C  W  Y  A  D  J  Y  B
I  A  B  B  P  C  H  K  E  D  U  Y  E  Q  S  Q  G  U  X  Y
I  B  U  Z  Z  A  H  O  X  M  M  M  B  E  K  J  V  I  R  U
L  B  R  J  Q  X  P  H  J  A  O  F  V  U  I  Q  X  N  C  G
Q  W  J  N  I  H  U  Z  J  L  A  B  P  U  U  U  Q  O  T  Q
O  B  S  A  I  Z  O  R  O  R  K  Y  Y  T  A  J  H  V  L  O
C  Z  P  L  A  M  T  H  D  N  R  O  R  A  L  P  H  F  H  T
Y  V  U  E  S  V  T  D  K  Y  D  G  V  Y  D  T  I  L  A  C
N  S  S  X  L  R  D  J  M  S  D  Y  V  M  L  Z  B  V  V  L
X  V  M  O  A  E  A  K  F  G  Z  A  L  X  B  P  P  K  V  O
K  I  U  B  P  V  T  A  P  Z  U  S  H  S  F  T  W  G  N  U
O  L  X  R  J  A  U  I  K  N  Y  G  O  W  F  T  D  W  V  I
V  U  B  Y  B  K  A  J  A  C  Z  L  K  D  R  H  S  X  B  I
W  P  J  P  G  D  R  K  F  H  U  F  V  U  P  P  B  O  R  F
```

POPULAR FEMALE NAMES IN 1777

Can you find these twelve popular female first names from 1777 in the grid below? **Answers on page 135.**

Bethiah	Hagar	Tamefin
Dorcas	Zipporah	Zibiah
Gillet	Lettice	Katura
Hepzibah	Mehitable	Damaris

```
E  S  Z  I  K  E  F  I  E  D  C  O  N  I  Z  A  H  B  V  C
G  L  F  I  Z  E  A  F  M  Y  C  T  X  V  Q  J  S  E  M  G
J  B  D  B  B  C  Z  N  E  F  O  T  L  Q  C  M  B  T  E  I
S  A  J  R  W  I  X  I  H  H  I  D  Y  H  E  Y  G  H  J  Y
Y  K  Z  X  A  F  A  W  I  E  G  M  Z  W  T  S  J  I  K  E
S  X  M  Q  G  F  T  H  T  S  C  P  F  S  X  E  G  A  N  W
Q  S  H  E  P  Z  I  B  A  H  N  I  W  U  M  X  Z  H  A  C
B  O  S  N  J  D  Y  C  B  R  P  N  T  A  M  E  F  I  N  E
F  I  R  V  A  H  R  N  L  X  O  D  Y  T  V  W  X  B  K  T
I  Q  K  R  C  O  O  X  E  J  N  P  N  Z  E  X  L  U  A  X
S  L  W  U  D  N  A  P  H  X  G  N  P  M  M  L  H  A  T  S
X  N  U  R  A  G  A  H  L  S  J  H  W  I  Z  L  I  Q  U  S
W  Q  E  X  N  P  Y  Q  V  P  J  T  N  L  Z  H  O  M  R  L
K  B  W  G  D  R  E  E  I  U  K  U  M  K  K  G  O  E  A  R
P  S  Y  X  Y  P  V  C  I  L  C  F  C  X  A  F  S  Z  M  F
Z  K  L  M  D  S  X  K  P  C  C  U  G  F  Q  Q  H  I  J  C
V  X  Z  Z  T  E  L  L  I  G  W  B  P  R  H  A  P  Y  L  Z
Q  E  E  Q  X  B  E  U  E  C  Q  D  A  M  A  R  I  S  R  M
K  O  A  V  Z  Y  Y  O  L  C  U  G  J  N  N  K  I  H  Y  F
M  O  A  M  S  I  B  C  R  W  A  G  U  B  H  C  E  N  A  E
```

FUNNY MONEY

Who do you think should be on our money?

And another featuring a cute puppy!

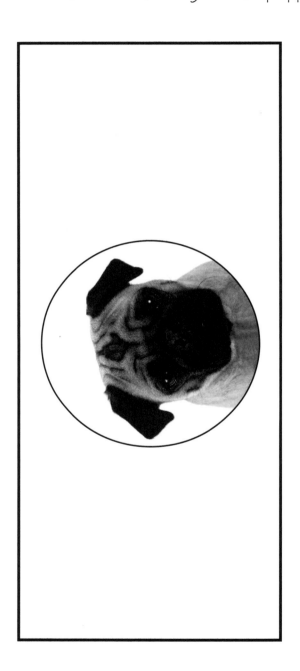

Now, create a piece of currency featuring our forty-fourth president, Barack Obama.

PRACTICE YOUR JOHN HANCOCK

The Declaration of Independence on the opposite page was signed by fifty-six members of the Continental Congress. These are the guys who told England they no longer had thirteen colonies in the Americas. Of these signers, most people only recall one of them: John Hancock, whose signature is so fancy and LARGE that his name is now a synonym for your signature. (As in, "Mom, put your John Hancock on this permission slip, please.")

What would your signature look like if you had to sign a very important document? Practice below.

A BIT OF LEARNIN'

Hancock's signature takes up 6.1 square inches of space (1.3 inches tall and 4.7 inches wide). The next-largest signature is only 3.4 square inches (William Ellery).

IN CONGRESS, JULY 4, 1776.
The unanimous Declaration of the thirteen united States of America,
IN CONGRESS

FOUR SCORE AND SEVEN YEARS AGO EQUALS . . . ?

In 1863, during the Civil War, President Abraham Lincoln delivered a short speech in Gettysburg, Pennsylvania, which was the scene of the Battle of Gettysburg, one of the most important battles of the war. The speech begins, "Four score and seven years ago, our fathers brought forth on this continent a new nation conceived in liberty and dedicated to the proposition that all men are created equal." The speech lasted just over two minutes, but it remains one of the best-known speeches in American history. But how long ago was four score and seven years? A score is twenty years, so four score (4 x 20) equals eighty years. Add seven and you have eighty-seven years ago, which in 1863 was 1776.

There are a lot of words that stand in for numbers. See how many of the math problems you can do below without looking at the hints. **Answers on page 136.**

1. Fortnight + 2 score = _____

2. A baker's dozen + goose egg – a brace = _____

3. A troika + a long score = _____

4. An Ogdoad – a tetrad = _____

5. 5 score x a fin = _____

6. 2 hexad + a gross = _____

7. A gross – a small gross = _____

8. A myriad – 5K = _____

9. A dozen + a heptad + a century = _____

10. Baker's dozen – banker's dozen = _____

11. Metric dozen + an ennead = _____

12. Half century / a brace = _____

13. Hexad x fin = _____

14. Metric dozen + banker's dozen + dozen + baker's dozen = _____

15. A gross / a dozen = _____

FOUR TETRADS AND SEVEN BRACES AGO?

Use the hints on the next page to come up with equations of your own. Try them out with your friends.

1.

_____

2.

_____

3.

_____

4.

_____

5.

_____

6.

_____

7.

_____

8.

_____

9.

_____

10.

_____

Hints

0	goose egg
2	brace
3	troika
4	tetrad
5	fin
6	hexad
7	heptad
8	Ogdoad
9	ennead
10	metric dozen
11	banker's dozen
12	dozen
13	baker's dozen
14	fortnight
20	score
21	long score
50	half century
100	century
120	small gross
144	gross
1,000	K
10,000	myriad

IT'S YOUR JOB: CAMPAIGN MANAGER

George Washington has traveled from the past and wants to run for president again. And he wants you to be his campaign manager! Come up with a slogan and some designs for the campaign buttons, hats, posters, and more on these pages.

RUN FOR IT!

Why don't **you** run for president? All you need is a knock-'em-dead campaign! Design it here.

TWO TRUTHS AND A LIE: AMERICAN HERO EDITION

Each of the following statements about an American hero has two correct answers. One is an outright lie. Can you find the fib? **Answers on page 136.**

1. George Washington...

  A) was born in 1732 in Virginia.
  B) never lived at the White House.
  C) would have hated this quiz because he never told a lie.

2. Harriet Tubman...

  A) was born into slavery but escaped.
  B) ran the New York City Railroad system.
  C) was a spy during the Civil War.

3. Charles Lindbergh...

  A) mysteriously disappeared while attempting to fly around the world.
  B) was the first person to fly a solo nonstop flight from the United States to Europe.
  C) left the United States after his son was kidnapped in what became the crime of the century.

4. Martin Luther King, Jr....

  A) believed in using nonviolent civil disobedience for racial equality.
  B) gave his most famous speech "I Had a Nightmare" in 1963.
  C) was assassinated in 1968.

5. Sacajawea . . .

A) helped Lewis and Clark during their historic exploration of the western United States in the early 1800s.
B) is featured on the US one-dollar coin.
C) welcomed the Pilgrims when they landed at Plymouth Rock.

6. Eleanor Roosevelt . . .

A) was President Theodore Roosevelt's daughter.
B) was the longest-serving First Lady in US history.
C) advocated for civil rights, women's rights, and workers' rights.

7. Susan B. Anthony . . .

A) played an important role in the women's suffrage movement (voting rights).
B) was the first women to cast a vote in a US election.
C) had the Nineteenth Amendment, giving women the right to vote, named after her: the Anthony Amendment.

8. George Washington Carver . . .

A) was George Washington's great-great-grandson.
B) was an African-American inventor and botanist whose work with crop rotation methods helped poor farmers improve the quality of their lives.
C) discovered up to three hundred uses for peanuts.

9. Thomas Edison . . .

A) held more than a thousand patents, including those for the phonograph, motion picture camera, and electric lightbulb.
B) only had three months of schooling because his teacher thought he was "addled."
C) wanted to call the lightbulb "Edison's Bright Idea."

10. Alexander Graham Bell . . .

A) had a knack for ventriloquism, which he would do at parties.
B) invented the first practical telephone.
C) was hard of hearing, which led to his greatest invention.

THE _____ MONUMENT

The Washington Monument is a 555-foot stone obelisk built to commemorate George Washington. The monument stands east of the Reflecting Pool and the Lincoln Memorial in Washington, DC. Design your own monuments on these pages to commemorate your favorite American, be it a president, Founding Father, your mom, or even your hamster.

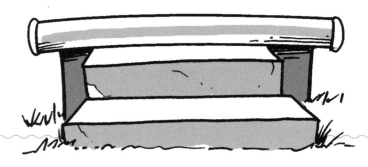

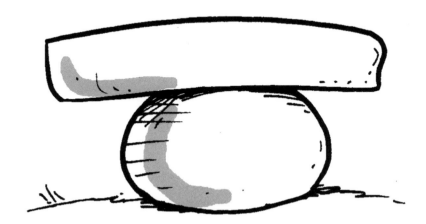

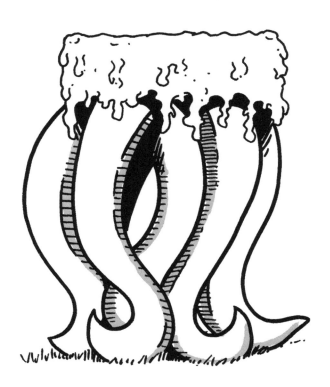

INITIAL THOUGHTS

The government has many agencies and departments working for the country. They usually have long names. In many cases, the first letter of each word in their names is used instead of having to say the whole name. For example, USA stands for *the United States (of) America*. These are called initialisms or acronyms.

What do these initialisms stand for? Many are US government agencies. Some are famous nongovernmental groups. One is just a person. Hint: *N* usually stands for *National*, *F* usually stands for *Federal*, and *D* usually stands for *Department*. **Answers on page 136.**

1. FBI

_____

2. CIA

_____

3. IRS

_____

4. NAACP

_____

5. LOC

_____

6. DOE

_____

7. AARP

_____

8. NASA

_____

9. NOAA

_____

10. NPR

_____

11. FDA

_____

12. FCC

_____

13. NPS

_____

14. WTO

_____

15. USMC

_____

16. USDA

_____

17. USCG

_____

18. USAF

_____

19. USPTO

_____

20. POTUS

_____

Sometimes initialisms create words. Take these normal words and come up with your own made-up departments or groups. For example: CAT = Crazy Americans (with) Tails.

DOG=

_____

BEG=

_____

NAP=

_____

HEAD=

_____

PRETTY=

_____

LICE=

_____

WORD=

_____

UNITE=

_____

USA=

_____

KANGAROO=

_____

TEAM DRAWING: THE US STATES EDITION

For this drawing game, you need two or more people, a pencil, and a map of the United States (like the one on the next page!). The object is to see if one player (the describer) can get the other (the drawer) to draw as accurately as possible one of the US states. The drawer cannot look at the map and must rely only on the describer's verbal directions. After the drawer is done, see if anyone can guess what state she drew. Then, switch places and try it again with another state.

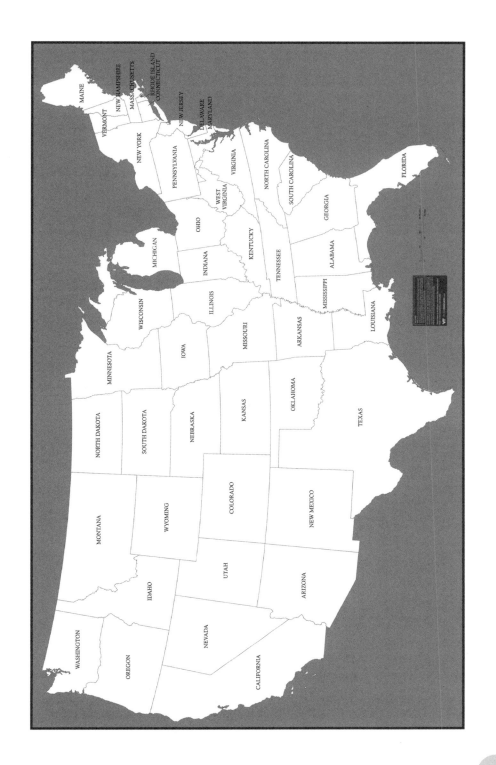

GOLD IN THEM THAR HILLS

In January 1848, James Marshall, a carpenter building a lumber mill in Coloma, California, discovered gold in the water wheel. Word spread quickly, and soon thousands went to California hoping to strike it rich. While most never found any gold, the rush helped settle California as a US state.

How much gold can you find in the grid on the next page?
Answers on page 137.

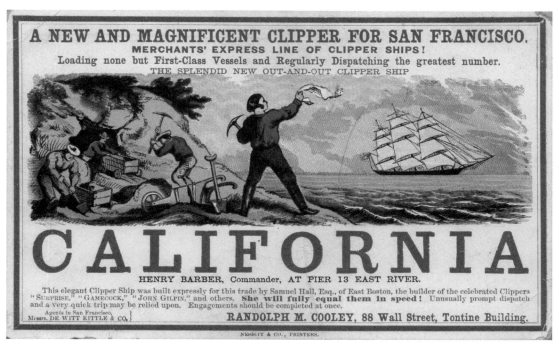

Courtesy of UC Berkeley, Bancroft Library

G	L	O	D	O	L	G	O	G	O	L	D	O	L	G
O	L	O	G	G	O	L	O	L	O	O	L	D	G	O
L	D	G	O	L	D	D	L	O	G	G	L	O	D	G
G	O	L	G	D	G	L	O	L	G	O	O	L	D	D
D	O	G	G	O	D	L	O	G	O	L	O	D	G	o
D	G	O	G	G	O	L	O	D	L	G	O	D	L	L
O	O	D	O	D	O	L	G	L	D	L	O	G	O	G
G	L	L	D	G	G	O	L	L	D	O	G	G	O	G
L	D	O	L	D	O	G	D	O	G	L	O	L	G	O
O	G	D	D	D	L	O	O	G	L	D	D	O	O	L
G	L	O	L	G	D	D	L	L	O	G	L	G	O	G
O	D	O	O	O	L	L	G	O	D	D	O	D	L	O
D	G	O	G	L	G	O	D	L	G	D	L	O	G	G
L	O	L	L	D	D	O	G	O	O	L	G	O	O	D
G	O	L	G	L	O	G	G	O	L	G	L	O	D	L

A BIT OF LEARNIN'

In 1846, San Francisco had around two hundred inhabitants. By 1852, after gold was discovered, thirty-six thousand people lived in the city!

MORE HAIR NEEDED

Abraham Lincoln wasn't the first president to sport a beard while in office; however, he did start a trend, as most of the presidents for the next fifty years had a mustache, a beard, or both. And now it's been more than a hundred years since America has elected a president with facial hair! Scientific research even proved that a mustache or beard makes it more difficult to get elected. Give the presidents on pages 68–70 some facial hair and see if you'd vote for them.

A BIT OF LEARNIN'

The last US president with facial hair was William Howard Taft (1909–1913).

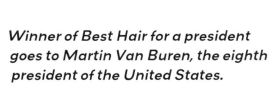

Winner of Best Hair for a president goes to Martin Van Buren, the eighth president of the United States.

Use these beards and mustaches for inspiration.

WHO WOULD YOU INVITE TO DINNER?

Who would you love to spend some time with? What would you talk about? Think of one notable American figure (alive or dead), one pop star, and one fictional character, and invite them to dinner. Use the space below to plan your meal, what you will talk about, and more. Use the space on the following page to write the conversation that would take place if you truly could invite these people to dinner.

Who would you invite and why?

1.

_____

2.

_____

3.

_____

What would you serve for dinner?

Appetizer:

_____

Main course:

_____

Dessert:

_____

What activities would you do after dinner?

_____

_____

_____

_____

What would you want to talk about at dinner?

_____

_____

_____

_____

What would you want to say to each of your dinner guests?

_____

_____

_____

_____

Create the dinner conversation here:

_____

_____

_____

_____

_____

_____

_____

HOW MANY . . .

Count 'em up! Answers on page 138.

. . . US presidents can you name?

_____

_____

_____

_____

_____

_____

_____

_____

_____

_____

_____

_____

. . . US states can you name?

_____

_____

_____

_____

_____

_____

_____

_____

. . . US state capitals can you name?

_____

_____

_____

_____

_____

_____

_____

_____

MINI CROSSWORDS

These bite-size nugget crosswords are great for when you only have a few minutes (or if you have little patience!). The only thing is, you have to figure out which boxes the answers to the clues belong in. **Answers on page 140.**

Founding Fathers' First Names

Clues
Adams
Franklin
Jefferson
Hamilton
Washington
Madison

Elements of the Flag

Clue
Colors and design
elements of America's flag

When It Happened

Clues
USA declares independence
We first land on the moon
Columbus finds "America"
World War II ends

First Ladies' First Names

Clues
Kennedy
Obama
Washington
Roosevelt (the second)
Clinton
Reagan
Madison
Lincoln

Independent Day

Clues
Words that have to do with the Fourth of July

WHAT WOULD . . .

Draw 'em as you see 'em!

... Abraham Lincoln's snowboard look like?

... America's national monster look like?

... America's national cartoon character look like?

... George Washington's lunch box look like?

. . . Thomas Jefferson look like if he were a frog?

. . . the Statue of Liberty look like if she were a warrior princess?

...an alien congressperson look like?

...the first Thanksgiving look like if they served octopus as the main dish?

OH, (VERB) CAN YOU (VERB) . . .

Our national anthem was written as a poem in 1814 by a lawyer after witnessing the bombing of Fort McHenry by British ships during the War of 1812. Over the years, Francis Scott Key's lyrics were set to music and became "The Star-Spangled Banner."

The lyrics below are missing some words. Read the missing parts of speech to a friend and have her fill in the blanks. Then try to sing the whole song without laughing!

Oh, say can you _____ by the dawn's early _____
           (VERB)   **(NOUN)**

What so _____ we hailed at the _____ last _____-ing?
         (ADVERB)   **(NOUN)**   **(VERB)**

Whose broad _____ and _____ stars thru the perilous _____,
       (PLURAL NOUN) (ADJECTIVE)   **(NOUN)**

O'er the _____ we _____ were so gallantly streaming?
     (PLURAL NOUN) (VERB [PAST TENSE])

And the _____' red _____, the bombs _____-ing in air,
     (PLURAL NOUN)   **(NOUN)**   **(VERB)**

Gave proof through the _____ that our _____ was still _____.
                    (NOUN)   **(NOUN)**   **(ADJECTIVE)**

Oh, say does that _____-_____ banner yet _____
            (NOUN) (ADJECTIVE)   (VERB)

O'er the land of the _____ and the home of the _____?
            (ADJECTIVE)   (ADJECTIVE)

Now sing your results!

Here's the original poem written in 1814. Only the first verse is used for the anthem.

Oh, say can you see by the dawn's early light
What so proudly we hailed at the twilight's last gleaming?
Whose broad stripes and bright stars thru the perilous fight,
O'er the ramparts we watched were so gallantly streaming?
And the rockets' red glare, the bombs bursting in air,
Gave proof through the night that our flag was still there.
Oh, say does that star-spangled banner yet wave
O'er the land of the free and the home of the brave?

On the shore, dimly seen through the mists of the deep,
Where the foe's haughty host in dread silence reposes,
What is that which the breeze, o'er the towering steep,
As it fitfully blows, half conceals, half discloses?
Now it catches the gleam of the morning's first beam,
In full glory reflected now shines in the stream:
'Tis the star-spangled banner! Oh long may it wave
O'er the land of the free and the home of the brave!

And where is that band who so vauntingly swore
That the havoc of war and the battle's confusion,
A home and a country should leave us no more!
Their blood has washed out their foul footsteps' pollution.
No refuge could save the hireling and slave

From the terror of flight, or the gloom of the grave:
And the star-spangled banner in triumph doth wave
O'er the land of the free and the home of the brave!

Oh! thus be it ever, when freemen shall stand
Between their loved home and the war's desolation!
Blest with victory and peace, may the heav'n rescued land
Praise the Power that hath made and preserved us a nation.
Then conquer we must, when our cause it is just,
And this be our motto: "In God is our trust."
And the star-spangled banner in triumph shall wave
O'er the land of the free and the home of the brave!

A BIT OF LEARNIN'

The War of 1812 was against the British, who,
though they were able to burn the White House
to the ground, were soon defeated in what was
called the second war of independence.

THE HUDDLED MASSES

Millions of people around the world came to America looking for a new life, and one of the first things they saw as they sailed into New York Harbor was the Statue of Liberty. A bronze plaque in its pedestal includes a poem by Emma Lazarus, with these famous lines: "Give me your tired, your poor, your huddled masses yearning to breathe free." Read the full poem below. Then think about your ancestors and how they came to America as you draw the "huddled masses" on the ship that brought them here on the next page.

THE NEW COLOSSUS

by Emma Lazarus

Not like the brazen giant of Greek fame,
With conquering limbs astride from land to land;
Here at our sea-washed, sunset gates shall stand
A mighty woman with a torch, whose flame
Is the imprisoned lightning, and her name
Mother of Exiles. From her beacon-hand
Glows world-wide welcome; her mild eyes command
The air-bridged harbor that twin cities frame.

"Keep, ancient lands, your storied pomp!" cries she
With silent lips. "Give me your tired, your poor,
Your huddled masses yearning to breathe free,
The wretched refuse of your teeming shore.
Send these, the homeless, tempest-tost to me,
I lift my lamp beside the golden door!"

Unless you are Native American, at least one of your ancestors emigrated to America.

HINKY PINKY CROSSWORD

A hinky pinky is a riddle where the answer is two rhyming words. For example, a purple gorilla is a grape ape. All the answers to this crossword puzzle are hinky pinkys.
Answers on page 140.

Across

1. Barack's mother
3. The United States and Soviet Union try to get to the moon first
6. President Clinton's pickles
9. Liberty ringer's outer shape
11. Franklin's writing utensils
12. Lady Liberty sneezes
13. New England locomotive
14. Martin Luther King's famous speech's main idea
15. The White House

Down

2. Lincoln's infants
4. How Alexander Hamilton died
5. Two brothers are the first to fly
7. Bird lawyer
8. Storage for the Stars and Stripes
10. Casting a ballot on the water

STATUES ARE FOR THE BIRDS

Here are some statues of famous Americans.
Draw birds on them.
Here's a quick lesson in drawing birds!

Amelia Earhart, Hollywood, California

Record-breaking aviator and pioneer who broke records for speed, altitude, and solo flight distances in the 1930s

Walt Disney and Mickey Mouse, Disneyland Park, Anaheim, California

Famous cartoonist, filmmaker, and creator of Mickey Mouse and many of his friends

Elvis Presley, Memphis, Tennessee

The King of rock and roll

Nathanael Greene, Greeneville, Tennessee

Revolutionary War general famous for his Southern campaign against the British

Frederick Douglass, Harlem, New York

An African-American social reformer, writer, orator, and statesman who escaped slavery and became a leader of the abolitionist movement

DON'T THINK TWICE: THE IMPORTANT YEARS EDITION

Answer the questions below as quickly as possible without putting too much thought into them. Time yourself and see how many you get right. Don't write in the book if you want to play with friends. **Answers on page 140.**

Scoring: Divide the number of seconds it took you to take the quiz by the number of questions you got correct. The lower your score, the better. For example, if it took you twenty seconds to get nine questions correctly answered, your score would be 2.2. If it took you twenty-five seconds to get all ten questions right, your score would be 2.5. So, in this case, speed was better than accuracy!

Hint: If you don't know an answer, skip it! Remember, the object of this quiz is not only to get as many correct answers as possible, but also to do it in as little time as possible.

1–3: Awesome!
4–6: Smarty-pants
7 & up: Not bad!

Fill in the blanks:

1. In _____, Columbus sailed the ocean blue.

2. The United States declared independence from Great Britain in _____.

3. In _____, gold was found in California, setting off a massive wave of settlers to the region.

4. In _____, the Civil War began.

5. In _____, Abraham Lincoln was assassinated as the Civil War drew to a close.

6. The Great Depression began in _____.

7. In _____, Japanese bombers attacked US ships at Pearl Harbor.

8. In _____, Neil Armstrong and Buzz Aldrin made the first moon landing.

9. In _____, Barack Obama was elected as the first African American president of the United States.

10. In _____, the US Senate approved the nomination of Sonia Sotomayor, the first Hispanic Supreme Court Justice.

THE RIGHT TO PROTEST

According to our Constitution, Americans are granted life, liberty, and the pursuit of happiness. Sometimes, however, we have to fight for particular freedoms, such as the right to be free from slavery, to be able to vote, to marry, and more. One way we fight for our freedoms is to protest. Famous Americans such as Martin Luther King, Jr., Rosa Parks, and Susan B. Anthony are great examples of people who have taken to the streets to voice their displeasure with how things are in order to bring about change. What are these people protesting?

FIELD GOAL

The first game of American football was played on November 6, 1869, between Rutgers and Princeton, two college teams. Today, football is the most popular sport in the United States.

Below is a goalpost with a football soaring through for three points. Can you move just two of the four poles to recreate the goalposts with the football on the outside? Use the following page to figure this out, or grab four pencils and an eraser to recreate the puzzle. **See answer on page 141.**

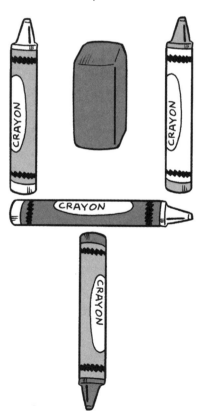

LIBERTY REIMAGINED

The Statue of Liberty was a gift to the United States from the people of France in 1886. The 151-foot statue represents freedom and liberty, and the woman is loosely based on Libertas, the ancient Roman goddess of freedom. The torch symbolizes progress, and the tablet she holds in her other hand represents law. The crown, enlightenment. Recreate the Statue of Liberty with your own symbols.

A BIT OF LEARNIN'

The tablet Lady Liberty holds is inscribed *July IV MDCCLXXVI*, which is July 4, 1776.

DON'T THINK TWICE: SPORTS EDITION

Answer the questions below as quickly as possible without putting too much thought into them. Time yourself and see how many you get right. Don't write in the book if you want to play with friends. *Answers on page 141.*

Scoring: Divide the number of seconds it took you to take the quiz by the number of questions you got correct. The lower your score, the better. For example, if it took you twenty seconds to get nine questions correctly answered, your score would be 2.2. If it took you twenty-five seconds to get all ten questions right, your score would be 2.5. So, in this case, speed was better than accuracy!

Hint: If you don't know an answer, skip it! Remember, the object of this quiz is not only to get as many correct answers as possible, but also to do it in as little time as possible.

1–3: Awesome!
4–6: Smarty-pants
7 & up: Not bad!

Fill in the blanks:

1. _____ is known as the national pastime.

2. _____ is the most watched sport in the United States.

3. The Major League Baseball championship is called the _____.

4. _____, which originally used two peach baskets as goals, was invented by James Naismith in 1891.

5. How many total players are on a soccer field (including both teams) during play? _____

6. Which major American sport doesn't use a ball? _____

7. The National Football League championship game is called the _____.

8. How many players are on the field in baseball? _____

9. _____ is the only sport that has been played on the moon.

10. _____ was the first African American to play Major League Baseball in the modern era.

STUFF WE LEFT ON THE MOON

One of the United States' greatest achievements was Apollo 11, the first manned mission to land on the moon, on July 20, 1969. But there have been plenty of other moon missions, some manned and others without astronauts. Since 1958, the United States and other countries have sent probes, crafts, and people to the moon, and we've left behind a lot of stuff—around two hundred tons of it!

Here's a partial list of our space garbage. Draw each object on the lunar surface on pages 124 and 125—can you get it all to fit?

A BIT OF LEARNIN'

Apollo 15 astronaut David Scott performed an experiment on the moon. He dropped a hammer and a feather at the same time in order to prove Galileo's theory that in the absence of atmosphere, objects will fall at the same rate no matter the mass. You can watch it here: bit.ly/1KLQzOB

- Footprints and rover tracks
- More than seventy spacecrafts
- Three Lunar Roving Vehicles
- Reflective panels called "lunar laser ranging retroreflector arrays"
- Five American flags
- Golf balls
- Twenty-four boots
- Magazines
- Ninety-six bags of spaceship garbage (food packages, pee and poop bags, etc.)
- Cameras
- Hammers
- Rakes
- Shovels
- Backpacks
- Blankets and towels
- Falcon feather
- Small three-inch sculpture commemorating men and women who died in pursuit of space travel
- Commemorative plaques
- Disk with goodwill message from world leaders
- Golden olive branch

AMERICAN FIRSTS

Can you guess how the following people changed history by being the first at something? There are clues hidden within each sentence if you need help. **Answers on page 141.**

1. Neil Armstrong's first was out of this world.

_____

2. Sally K. Ride's first was also out of this world.

_____

3. Edith Wharton's first was certainly novel.

_____

4. Jeanette Piccard may have had an inflated ego after her first.

_____

5. Samoset ran into a bunch of thankful strangers.

_____

6. Jackie Robinson knocked it out of the park.

_____

7. All Virginia Dare had to do to achieve her first was get born.

_____

8. Sandra Day O'Connor's first was quite an honor.

_____

9. Charles Lindbergh achieved this first by going and going and going.

_____

10. Amelia Earhart achieved her first by following in Lindbergh's footsteps.

---

11. Annie Edson Taylor had a barrel of laughs over her first.

---

12. Barack Obama's first led the nation.

---

13. Victoria Woodhull didn't have to win for her first—she only had to run.

---

14. Henry Ford's first was a gas.

---

15. Thomas Burke's first was golden.

---

16. Orville and Wilbur Wright's first was for the birds.

---

17. Thurgood Marshall used a gavel to break the color barrier.

---

18. Elizabeth Blackwell's first required a lot of patients.

---

19. Booker T. Washington was the first African American mail.

---

20. Chuck Yeager was so fast that his first broke a record . . . and something else.

MOUNT _____-MORE

Mount Rushmore, located near Keystone, South Dakota, is a carved sculpture of four US presidents: George Washington, Thomas Jefferson, Theodore Roosevelt, and Abraham Lincoln. Who do you think belongs carved in stone? Draw them as you think they should look!

A BIT OF LEARNIN'

Each of the heads in Mount Rushmore is about sixty-five feet tall.

Your favorite cartoon characters?

Your favorite animals?

Your family?

Your pets?

Aliens and monsters?

What else you can think of?

AMERICA IS FUNNY

Do you know the answers to these patriotic puzzlers?
Answers on page 142.

1. What is the capital of Washington?

_____

2. Why can't a woman living in the United States be buried in Canada?

_____

3. What US state is round on the ends and high in the middle?

_____

4. What do you call doing two thousand pounds of laundry?

_____

5. What did one US flag say to the other?

_____

6. What is the smartest state?

_____

7. What would you call the United States if everyone had a pink car?

_____

8. Where was the Declaration of Independence signed?

_____

9. What state needs a tissue?

_____

10. What state is the bandage state?

_____

11. Why does the Mississippi River see so well?

_____

12. What rock group has four guys who don't sing?

_____

13. What did the Americans do because of the Stamp Act?

_____

14. What kind of music did the Pilgrims like?

_____

15. What kind of tea did the American colonists want?

_____

The Oval Office is the president's office in the West Wing of the White House. Newly elected presidents can redecorate the room. It's your job to help!

UNITED PUNS OF AMERICA

Each of the blanks in the sentences can be completed using the name of one of the states in the United States. For instance: I dropped my paddle; now I will have to pick up my OREGON (oar again). Stumped? Turn the book upside down to read the hints! **Answers on page 145, and use the list of US states on page 139 to help you figure out the tough ones.**

1. Abe: Does Suzy want to go to the store?
Mary: I don't know _____.

Hint: It's our largest state and over twice the size of Texas.

2. George: What did _____ to the party?
Martha: She wore a new dress.

Hint: It was the first state to ratify the US Constitution.

3. My sister lent me $2,000 and now _____ a lot of money.

Hint: It's the only state name that starts with two vowels.

4. I would love a cola, but I'm not very thirsty, so I'll just have a _____.

Hint: This midwestern state's capital is St. Paul.

5. _____ loves company.

Hint: This midwestern state is known as the Show-Me State.

6. The football player ruined his uniform and now he needs a _____.

Hint: This state is known as the Garden State.

7. That dog's name is Ari. Who is _____?

Hint: This state's capital is Phoenix.

8. I bet _____ wood faster than you can.

Hint: This southern state's capital is Little Rock.

9. Hurry up! I don't want to miss the _____ event!

Hint: This state in New England is the most eastern in the United States and is the only state whose name has one syllable.

10. Bill: What did _____?
Hillary: Her garden, of course!

Hint: This state in the Northwest is sometimes known as the Potato State.

11. What a wonderful visit. When _____ you again?

Hint: This southeastern state is famous for its country music.

12. I have two strikes, but I promise I won't _____.

Hint: Located in the Great Lakes region, this state's largest city is Detroit.

13. John: _____?
Abigail: I'm fine. How are you?

Hint: This was the last state admitted to the Union.

14. Franklin: _____ come out and play?
Eleanor: Sorry, Tucky has homework to do.

Hint: This is known as the Bluegrass State.

PERSONALITY STATES

Give the states on the following pages some personality by giving them faces, arms, and legs.

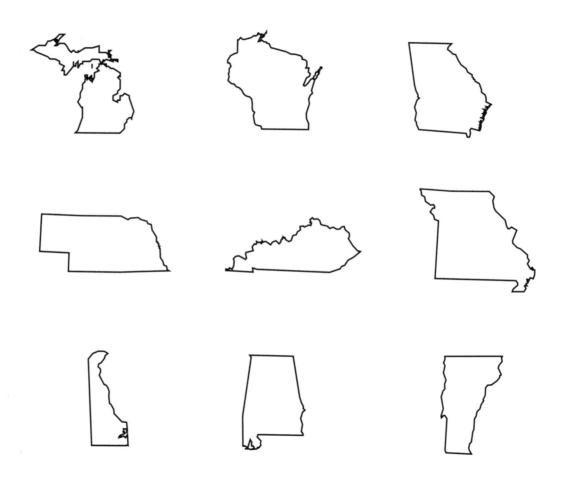

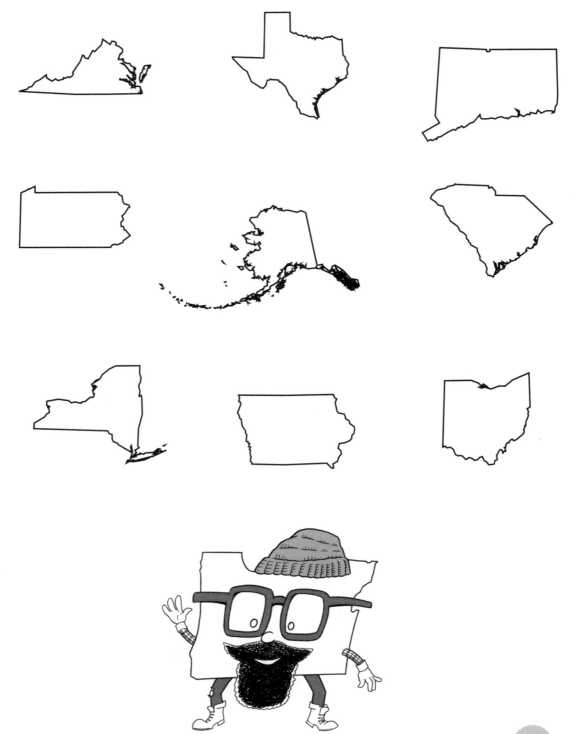

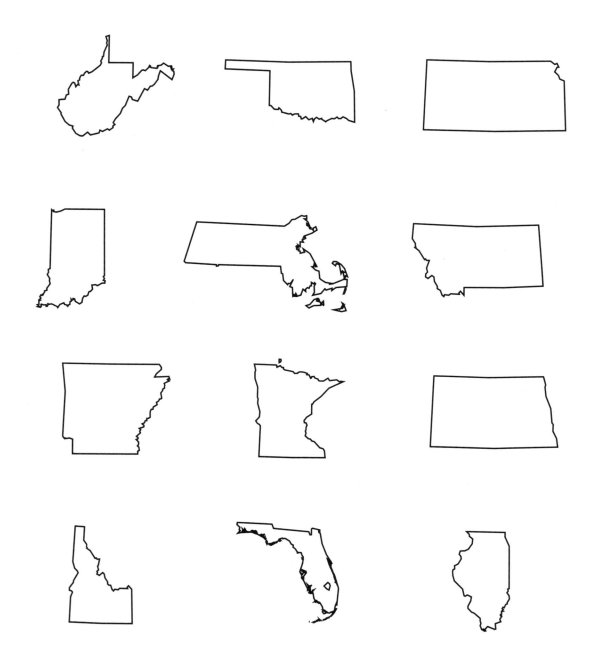

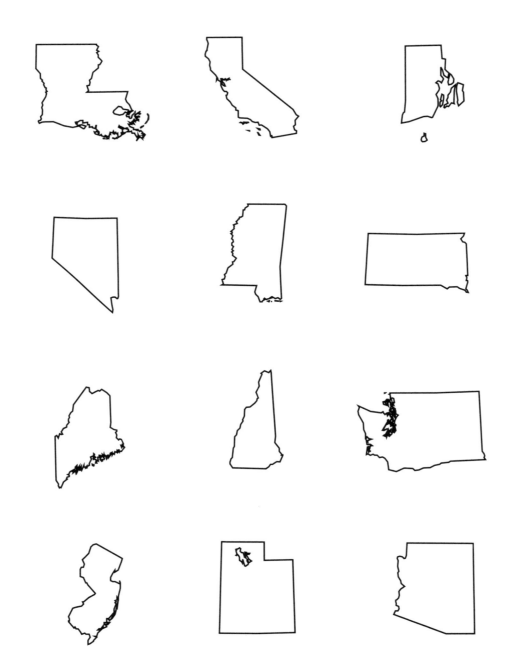

FILL 'ER UP

The Grand Canyon in Arizona is 277 miles long, up to 18 miles wide, and over a mile deep at its deepest point. About five million tourists visit this natural wonder every year.

How many gummy bears would it take to fill up the Grand Canyon? Draw it to find out! Or you could fill it up with balls. Or teddy bears. Bicycle wheels? Whatever you want!

HOW AMERICAN ARE YOU?

The easiest way to become an American citizen is to be born in the United States. But noncitizen legal residents of the United States can apply to become citizens. This process includes a ten-question test, which you have to answer out loud. In order to pass, you have to get six out of ten correct. The ten questions come from a large pool of one hundred possible options. Test your knowledge of your country by taking this quiz of thirty of those questions. In order to pass, you need to answer eighteen correctly. **Answers on page 143.**

American Government

1. What is the supreme law of the land?

_____

2. What stops a single branch of government from becoming too powerful?

_____

3. Who is in charge of the executive branch?

_____

4. What is the highest court in the United States?

_____

5. What do we call the first ten amendments to the Constitution?

_____

6. What is one right or freedom from the First Amendment? (More than one answer)

_____

7. What did the Declaration of Independence do?

_____

8. What is one right in the Declaration of Independence? (More than one answer)

_____

9. What are the two major political parties in the United States?

_____

10. Who is the commander in chief of the military?

_____

American History

11. Why did the colonists fight the British?

_____

12. Who wrote the Declaration of Independence?

_____

13. There were thirteen original states. Name three.

_____

14. What is one thing Benjamin Franklin is famous for?

_____

15. What territory did the United States buy from France in 1803?

_____

16. Name one problem that led to the Civil War.

_____

17. What did the Emancipation Proclamation do?

_____

18. What did Susan B. Anthony do?

_____

19. Who was president during the Great Depression and World War II?

_____

20. What movement tried to end racial discrimination?

_____

Civics

21. Name one of the two longest rivers in the United States.

_____

22. What ocean is on the West Coast of the United States?

_____

23. What ocean is on the East Coast of the United States?

_____

24. Name one US territory.

_____

25. Name one state that borders Canada.

_____

26. Name one state that borders Mexico.

_____

27. What is the capital of the United States?

_____

28. Why does the flag have thirteen stripes?

_____

29. Why does the flag have fifty stars?

_____

30. What is the name of the national anthem?

_____

All About America (page 6)

1. The United States of America; 2. The United States, America, the USA, the US; 3. 1776; 4. July 4; 5. Any of the Founding Fathers (or Mothers); 6. 50 (states); 7. Mexico to the south and Canada to the north; 8. "The Star-Spangled Banner" (national anthem); 9. Uncle Sam (symbol of the US government); 10. Bald eagle (national bird); 11. Rose (national flower); 12. All the way to the moon; 13. Oak (national tree)

Don't Think Twice: Founding Fathers Edition (page 10)

1. George; 2. Adams; 3. Jefferson; 4. Hancock; 5. Franklin; 6. Hamilton; 7. Madison; 8. John; 9. Henry; 10. Adams

States of Confusion (page 16)

1. New York; 2. Wyoming (willing to accept Colorado!); 3. Massachusetts; 4. Idaho; 5. Ohio; 6. Texas; 7. Connecticut; 8. Maine; 9. Maryland; 10. Montana; 11. Alaska; 12. New Jersey; 13. Louisiana; 14. Florida; 15. Virginia; 16. California

Abbreviation Completion (page 18)

(You probably found other correct answers—yours are just as good as these!)

1. **WA**shington pledged a sole**MN** oath to defend the **FL**edgling nation. **FOR**eign nations that interfered **WI**th US **MA**tters would **PA**y the p**RI**ce.

2. On November 2, 1983, President Ron**AL**d Reagan signed a bill **DE**claring the third **MO**nday of Janu**AR**y a holiday honoring Martin **LUT**her **KIN**g, Jr.

3. Tha**T X**erox mac**HI**ne te**ND**s to break down just when I need to m**AK**e a lot of **CO**pies.

4. My **SC**hool's impro**V T**heater a**CT**ing v**ID**eo gained ma**NY** ne**W** Viewers **LA**st week.

5. By **MI**dnight the only o**NE**s left at the **VACA**tion home were Mo**M**, **D**ad, and **ME**.

6. Tommy'**S D**entist administered a ne**W**, **V**ery painful procedure. It made him **IL**l and d**AZ**ed, and now he can only lic**K Y**ogurt for the rest of the day.

7. **ON** Cold days, **I A**lways enjoy the war**MT**h of **JOH**n's billo**WY** gree**N J**acket. He asks me not to, but then he says, "**OK**ay."

8. Whiskers squir**MS** until I give him his ca**TN**ap toy. He i**NH**ales it and then lies there u**NM**oving.

Popular Male Names in 1777 (page 35)

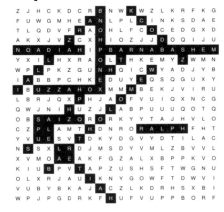

Popular Female Names in 1777 (page 36)

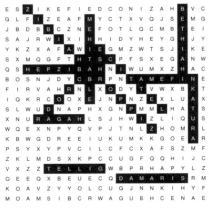

Four Score and Seven Years Ago Equals . . . ? (page 44)

1. 54; 2. 11; 3. 24; 4. 4; 5. 500; 6. 156; 7. 24; 8. 5,000; 9. 119; 10. 2; 11. 19; 12. 25; 13. 30; 14. 46; 15. 12

Two Truths and a Lie: American Hero Edition (page 52)

1. C: Just like everyone else, Washington probably told a fib or two. The cherry tree myth was first written in a biography ten years after Washington's death, and there is no proof it ever happened.
2. B: Harriet Tubman used a network of safe houses known as the Underground Railroad to help slaves escape their masters. This was not a real railroad, however.
3. A: Aviator Amelia Earhart disappeared during her attempt to fly around the world in 1939.
4. B: King's most famous speech was called "I Have a Dream."
5. C: You may have been thinking of Squanto, who helped the Pilgrims after their first winter in the New World.
6. A: She was niece to President Theodore Roosevelt, not daughter. Her husband, Franklin D. Roosevelt, was her fifth cousin once removed.
7. B: The Nineteenth Amendment, giving women the right to vote, wasn't ratified until 1920, fourteen years after Anthony's death.
8. A: Carver gave himself the middle name "Washington" and wasn't related to the first president.
9. C: The lightbulb *was* a bright idea, but Edison didn't call it that.
10. C: Bell's mother's deafness led him to study acoustics, which eventually led to the telephone.

Initial Thoughts (page 58)

1. Federal Bureau of Investigation; 2. Central Intelligence Agency; 3. Internal Revenue Service; 4. National Association for the Advancement of Colored People; 5. Library of Congress; 6. Department of Energy; 7. American Association of Retired Persons; 8. National Aeronautics and Space Administration; 9. National Oceanic and Atmospheric Administration; 10. National Public Radio; 11. Food (and) Drug Administration; 12. Federal Communications

Commission; 13. National Park Service; 14. World Trade Organization; 15. United States Marine Corps; 16. United States Department of Agriculture; 17. United States Coast Guard; 18. United States Air Force; 19. United States Patent and Trademark Office; 20. President of the United States

Gold in Them Thar Hills (page 64)

"Gold" appears thirteen times in the puzzle.

G	L	O	D	O	L	G	O	**G**	**O**	**L**	**D**	O	L	G
O	L	O	G	G	O	L	O	L	O	O	L	D	G	O
L	D	**G**	**O**	**L**	**D**	D	L	O	G	G	L	O	D	G
G	O	L	G	D	G	L	O	L	**G**	O	O	L	D	D
D	O	G	G	O	**D**	**L**	**O**	**G**	**O**	L	O	D	G	o
D	**G**	O	G	G	O	L	O	D	**L**	G	O	D	L	L
O	**O**	D	O	D	O	L	G	L	**D**	**L**	**O**	**G**	O	**G**
G	**L**	L	D	G	**G**	O	L	L	D	O	G	G	**O**	G
L	**D**	O	L	D	**O**	**G**	D	O	G	L	O	**L**	G	O
O	G	D	**D**	**D**	**L**	**O**	**O**	G	L	D	**D**	O	O	L
G	L	O	**L**	**G**	**D**	D	L	**L**	O	G	L	G	O	G
O	D	**O**	**O**	**O**	L	L	G	O	**D**	D	O	D	L	O
D	**G**	O	**G**	**L**	G	O	D	L	G	**D**	**L**	**O**	**G**	G
L	O	L	L	**D**	D	O	G	O	O	L	G	O	O	D
G	O	L	G	L	O	G	G	O	L	G	L	O	D	L

How Many . . . (page 74)

US Presidents

1. George Washington, 1789–1797
2. John Adams, 1797–1801
3. Thomas Jefferson, 1801–1809
4. James Madison, 1809–1817
5. James Monroe, 1817–1825
6. John Quincy Adams, 1825–1829
7. Andrew Jackson, 1829–1837
8. Martin Van Buren, 1837–1841
9. William Henry Harrison, 1841
10. John Tyler, 1841–1845
11. James Knox Polk, 1845–1849
12. Zachary Taylor, 1849–1850
13. Millard Fillmore, 1850–1853
14. Franklin Pierce, 1853–1857
15. James Buchanan, 1857–1861
16. Abraham Lincoln, 1861–1865
17. Andrew Johnson, 1865–1869
18. Ulysses S. Grant, 1869–1877
19. Rutherford Birchard Hayes, 1877–1881
20. James Abram Garfield, 1881
21. Chester Alan Arthur, 1881–1885
22. Grover Cleveland, 1885–1889
23. Benjamin Harrison, 1889–1893
24. Grover Cleveland, 1893–1897
25. William McKinley, 1897–1901
26. Theodore Roosevelt, 1901–1909
27. William Howard Taft, 1909–1913
28. Woodrow Wilson, 1913–1921
29. Warren Gamaliel Harding, 1921–1923
30. Calvin Coolidge, 1923–1929
31. Herbert Clark Hoover, 1929–1933
32. Franklin Delano Roosevelt, 1933–1945
33. Harry S. Truman, 1945–1953
34. Dwight David Eisenhower, 1953–1961
35. John Fitzgerald Kennedy, 1961–1963
36. Lyndon Baines Johnson, 1963–1969
37. Richard Milhous Nixon, 1969–1974
38. Gerald Rudolph Ford, 1974–1977
39. James Earl Carter, Jr., 1977–1981
40. Ronald Wilson Reagan, 1981–1989
41. George Herbert Walker Bush, 1989–1993
42. William Jefferson Clinton, 1993–2001
43. George Walker Bush, 2001–2009
44. Barack Hussein Obama, 2009–

US States and Their Capitals

Alabama: Montgomery
Alaska: Juneau
Arizona: Phoenix
Arkansas: Little Rock
California: Sacramento
Colorado: Denver
Connecticut: Hartford
Delaware: Dover
Florida: Tallahassee
Georgia: Atlanta
Hawaii: Honolulu
Idaho: Boise
Illinois: Springfield
Indiana: Indianapolis
Iowa: Des Moines
Kansas: Topeka
Kentucky: Frankfort
Louisiana: Baton Rouge
Maine: Augusta
Maryland: Annapolis
Massachusetts: Boston
Michigan: Lansing
Minnesota: St. Paul
Mississippi: Jackson
Missouri: Jefferson City
Montana: Helena
Nebraska: Lincoln
Nevada: Carson City
New Hampshire: Concord
New Jersey: Trenton
New Mexico: Santa Fe
New York: Albany
North Carolina: Raleigh
North Dakota: Bismarck
Ohio: Columbus
Oklahoma: Oklahoma City
Oregon: Salem

Pennsylvania: Harrisburg
Rhode Island: Providence
South Carolina: Columbia
South Dakota: Pierre
Tennessee: Nashville
Texas: Austin
Utah: Salt Lake City
Vermont: Montpelier
Virginia: Richmond
Washington: Olympia
West Virginia: Charleston
Wisconsin: Madison
Wyoming: Cheyenne

Mini Crosswords (page 76)

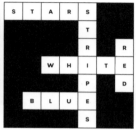
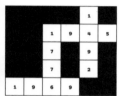

Hinky Pinky Crossword (page 90)

Across

1. Obama mama; 3. space race; 6. Bill's dills; 9. bell shell;
11. Ben's pens; 12. statue achoo; 13. Maine train; 14. dream theme;
15. presidents' residence

Down

2. Abe's babes, 4. cruel duel, 5. Wright flight, 7. legal eagle, 8. flag bag,
10. boat vote

Don't Think Twice: The Important Years Edition (page 98)

1. 1492; 2. 1776; 3. 1848; 4. 1861; 5. 1865; 6. 1929; 7. 1941; 8. 1969;
9. 2008; 10. 2009

Field Goal (page 102)

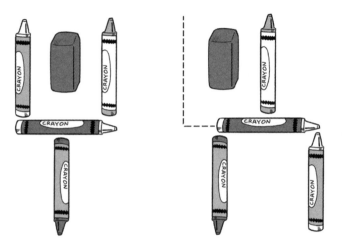

Move the top left goal post to the bottom right and shift the middle crayon to the right.

Don't Think Twice: Sports Edition (page 106)
1. Baseball; 2. Football; 3. World Series; 4. Basketball; 5. Twenty-two; 6. Hockey; 7. Super Bowl; 8. Nine; 9. Golf; 10. Jackie Robinson

American Firsts (page 112)
1. Neil Armstrong was the first man to step foot on the moon, on July 20, 1969.
2. Sally Ride was the first American woman in space, on June 18, 1983.
3. Edith Wharton was the first woman to win a Pulitzer Prize for fiction in 1920 (for her book *The Age of Innocence*).
4. Jeanette Piccard was the first woman to travel fifty-seven thousand feet in a hot air balloon—setting a record in 1934.
5. Samoset was the first Native American to make contact with the Pilgrims of Plymouth Colony, in 1621.
6. Jackie Robinson was the first African American to break into (until then) all-white Major League Baseball, in 1947.
7. Virginia Dare was the first person born in America to English parents, in 1587 (Roanoke Island, Virginia).
8. Sandra Day O'Connor was the first female US Supreme Court justice, serving from 1981 until 2006.

9. Charles Lindbergh was the first person to fly nonstop from the United States to Europe, in 1927.

10. Amelia Earhart was the first female aviator to fly solo across the Atlantic Ocean, in 1928.

11. In 1901, Annie Edson Taylor became the first person to go over Niagara Falls in a barrel and survive.

12 Barack Obama was the first African American president of the United States.

13. Victoria Woodhull was the first woman to run for president, in 1872—long before women could even vote!

14. Although Henry Ford didn't invent the automobile, his Model T (introduced in 1908) became the first affordable motor car, opening travel to middle-class Americans.

15. Thomas Burke won the first Olympic gold medals for the United States, in the 1896 Olympic Games (the first modern Olympics).

16. The Wright brothers invented and built the world's first successful airplane, in 1903.

17. Thurgood Marshall was the first African American Supreme Court judge, serving from 1967 until 1991.

18. Elizabeth Blackwell was the first woman in the United States to receive a medical degree, in 1849.

19. Booker T. Washington was the first African American to appear on a US postage stamp, in 1940.

20. Chuck Yeager was the first person to break the sound barrier by flying faster than the speed of sound, in 1947.

America Is Funny (page 118)

1. W; 2. Because she's still alive; 3. Ohio; 4. Washing-ton; 5. Nothing, it just waved; 6. Alabama—it has four A's and one B; 7. A pink carnation; 8. At the bottom; 9. Mass-*ACHOO*-setts; 10. Connect-a-cut; 11. Because it has four I's; 12. Mount Rushmore; 13. They licked the British; 14. Plymouth Rock; 15. Liberty

United Puns of America (page 122)

1. Alaska (*I'll ask her*); 2. Delaware (*Della wear*); 3. Iowa (*I owe her*); 4. Minnesota (*mini soda*); 5. Missouri (*Misery*); 6. New Jersey (*exactly what it says!*); 7. Arizona (*Ari's owner*); 8. Arkansas (*I can saw*); 9. Maine (*main*); 10. Idaho (*Ida hoe*); 11. Tennessee (*can I see you*); 12. Michigan (miss again); 13. Hawaii (How are you); 14. Kentucky (*Can Tucky*)

How American Are You? (page 130)

1. The Constitution; 2. Checks and balances (separation of powers); 3. The president; 4. The Supreme Court; 5. The Bill of Rights; 6. Speech, religion, assembly, press, petition the government; 7. Announced our independence from Great Britain; 8. Life, liberty, pursuit of happiness; 9. Democratic and Republican; 10. The president; 11. Because of high taxes (taxation without representation), the British army stayed in their houses (boarding, quartering), and because they didn't have self-government; 12. Thomas Jefferson; 13. New Hampshire, Massachusetts, Rhode Island, Connecticut, New York, New Jersey, Pennsylvania, Delaware, Maryland, Virginia, North Carolina, South Carolina, Georgia; 14. US diplomat, oldest member of the Constitutional Convention, first Postmaster General of the United States, writer of *Poor Richard's Almanack*, started the first free libraries; 15. The Louisiana Territory; 16. Slavery, economic reasons, states' rights; 17. Freed the slaves; 18. Fought for women's rights and civil rights; 19. Franklin D. Roosevelt; 20. Civil Rights Movement; 21. Missouri River, Mississippi River; 22. Pacific Ocean; 23. Atlantic Ocean; 24. Puerto Rico, US Virgin Islands, American Samoa, Northern Mariana Islands, Guam; 25. Maine, New Hampshire, Vermont, New York, Pennsylvania, Ohio, Michigan, Minnesota, North Dakota, Montana, Idaho, Washington, Alaska; 26. California, Arizona, New Mexico, Texas; 27. Washington, DC; 28. There were thirteen original colonies; 29. There is one star for each state; 30. The Star-Spangled Banner